Piano Solo

SONGS WITH A
CLASSICAL TOUCH

ISBN 978-1-4950-0683-8

HAL•LEONARD®
CORPORATION

7777 W. BLUEMOUND RD. P.O. BOX 13819 MILWAUKEE, WI 53213

Visit Hal Leonard Online at
www.halleonard.com

Contents

ALSO SPRACH ZARATHUSTRA

featured in the Motion Picture 2001: A SPACE ODYSSEY

By RICHARD STRAUSS

Moderately

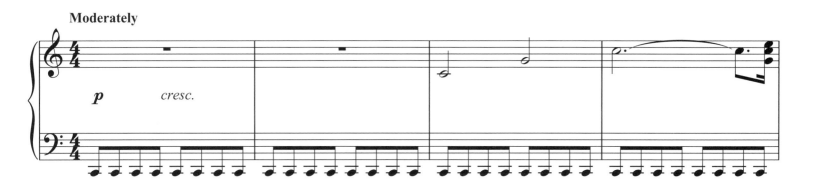

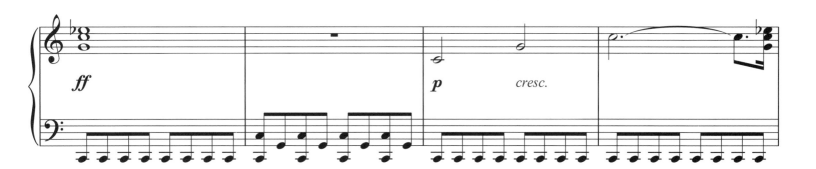

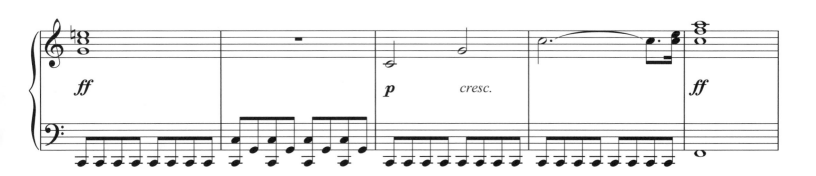

BLUE TANGO

By LEROY ANDERSON

THE BELLE OF THE BALL

By LEROY ANDERSON

Allegro animato (♩. = 88)

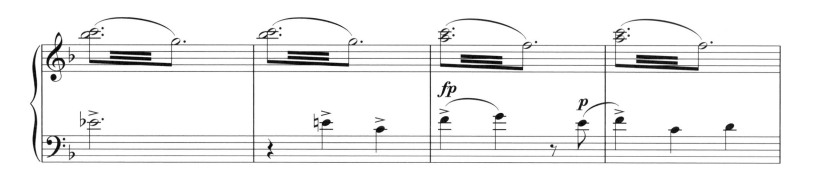

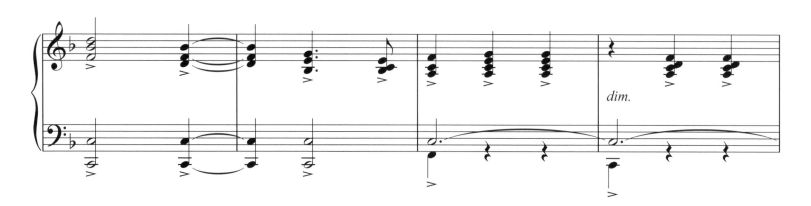

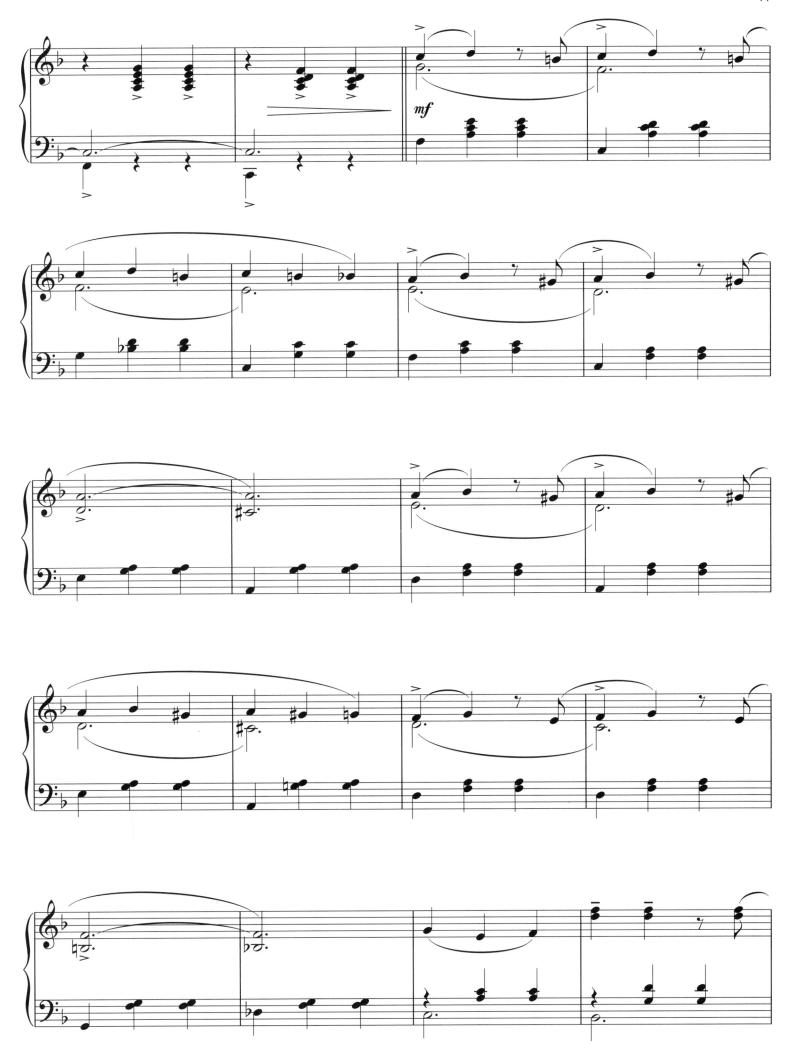

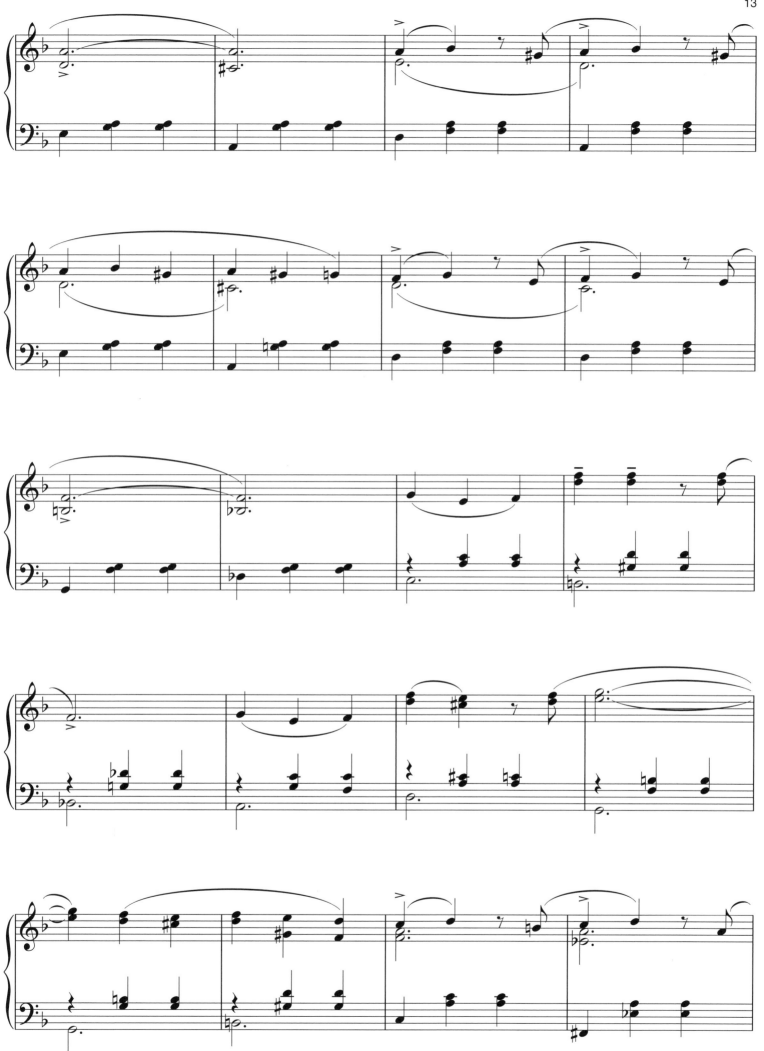

15

BUGLER'S DREAM
(Olympic Fanfare)

By LEO ARNAUD

Moderate March tempo

A little faster

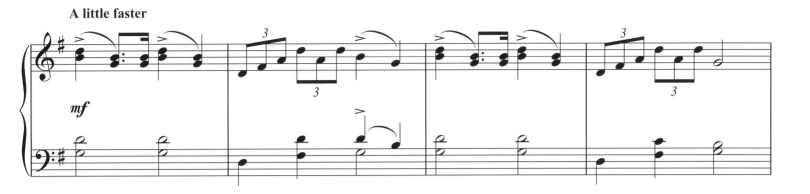

THEME FROM CLOSE ENCOUNTERS
OF THE THIRD KIND

By JOHN WILLIAMS

CAVATINA
from the Universal Pictures and EMI Films Presentation THE DEER HUNTER

By STANLEY MYERS

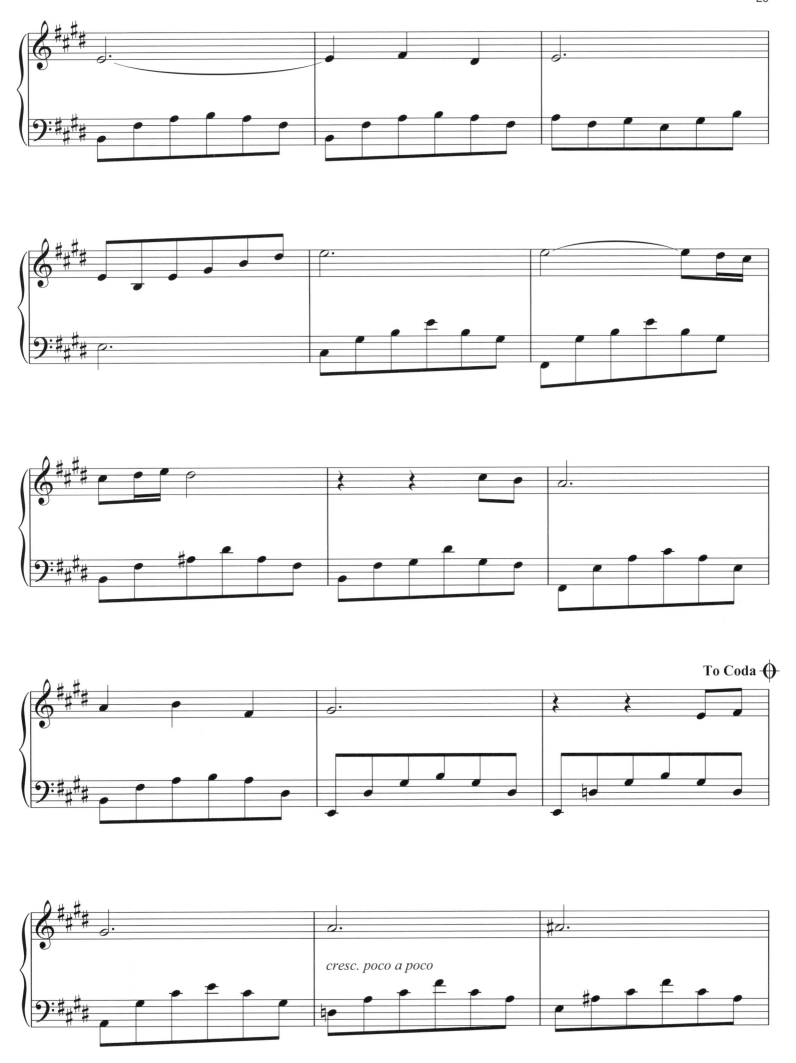

To Coda ⊕

cresc. poco a poco

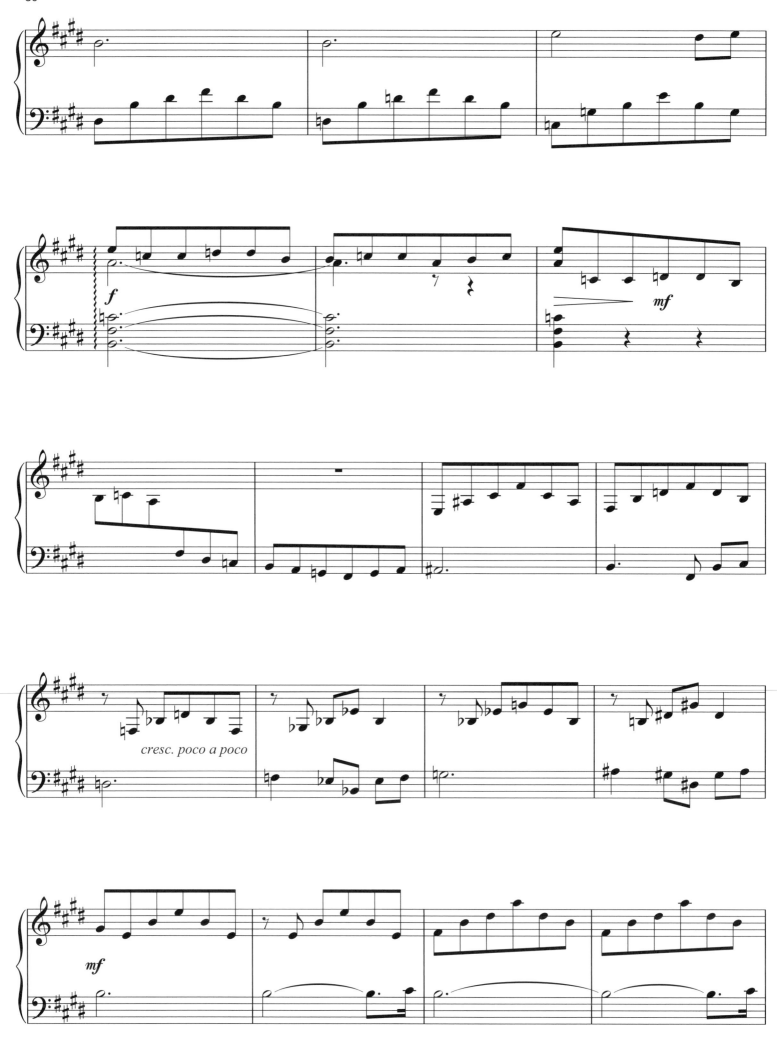

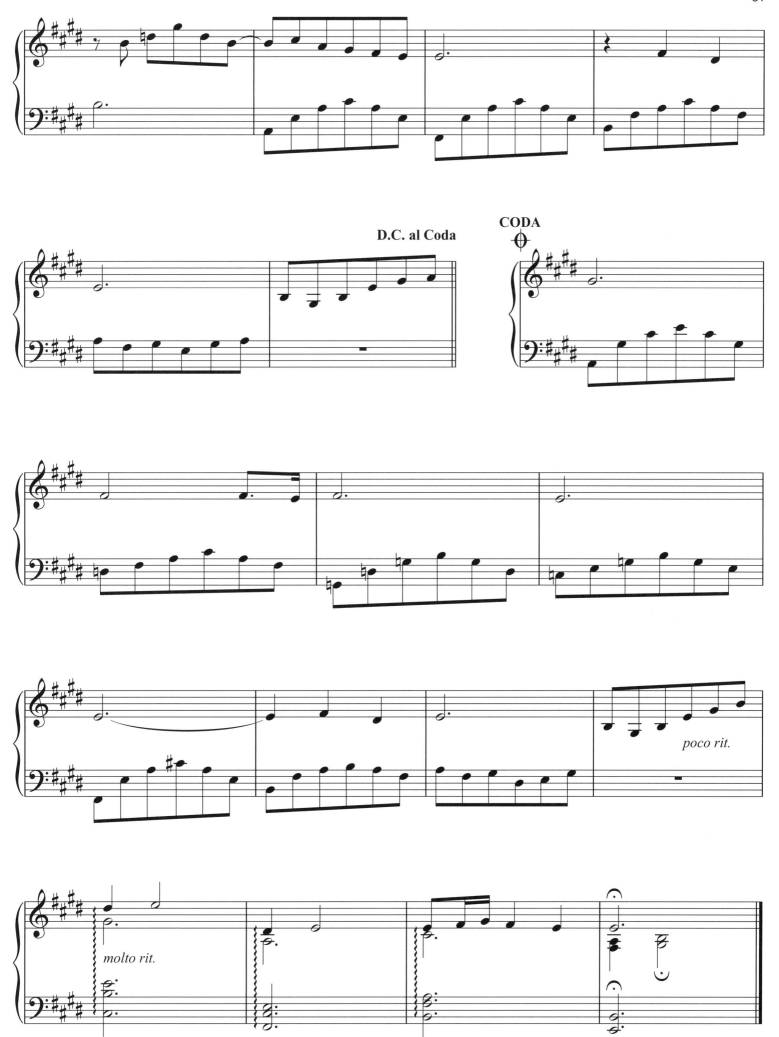

CINDERELLA WALTZ
from CINDERELLA

Music by RICHARD RODGERS

Tempo di Waltz

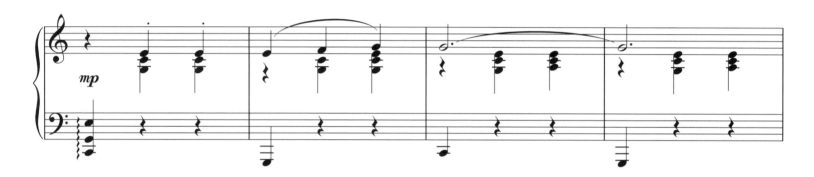

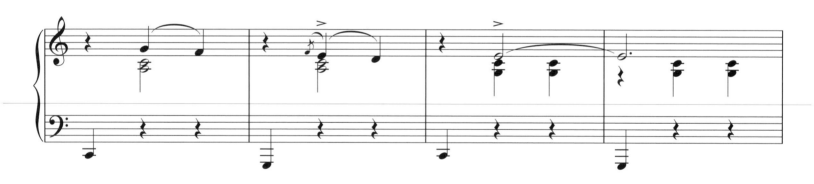

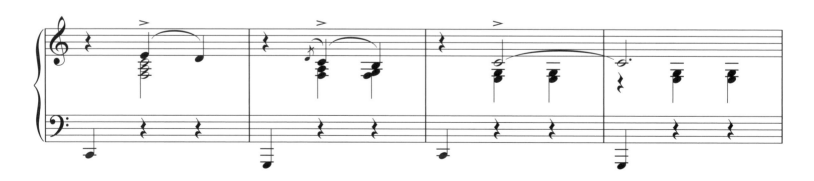

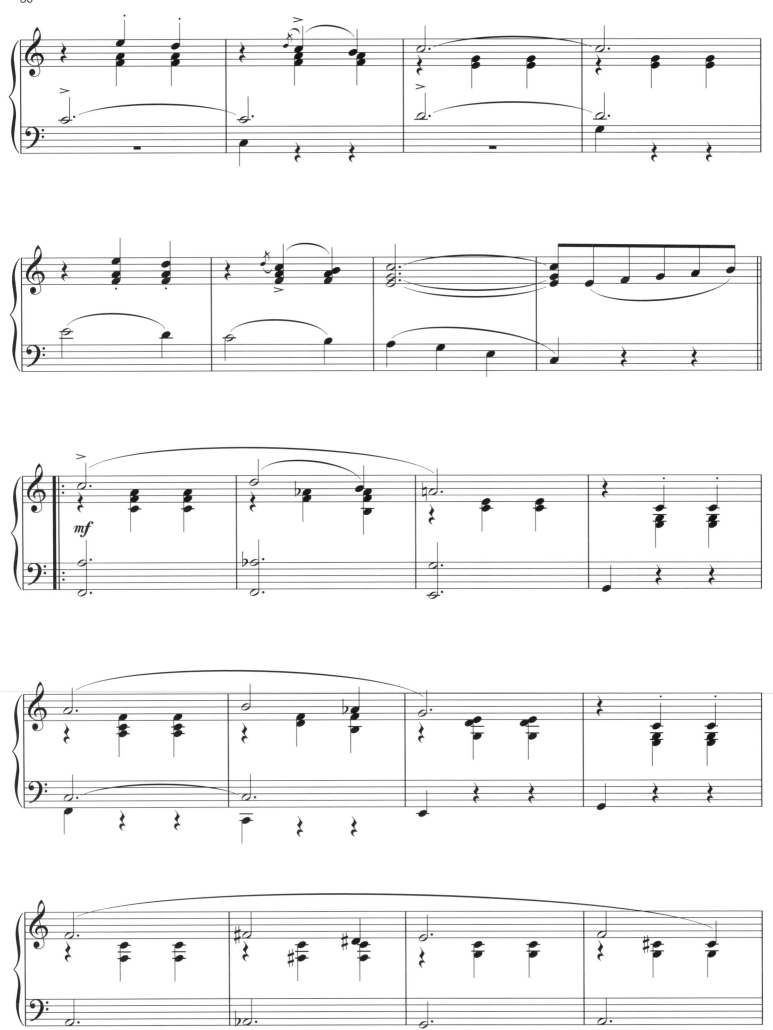

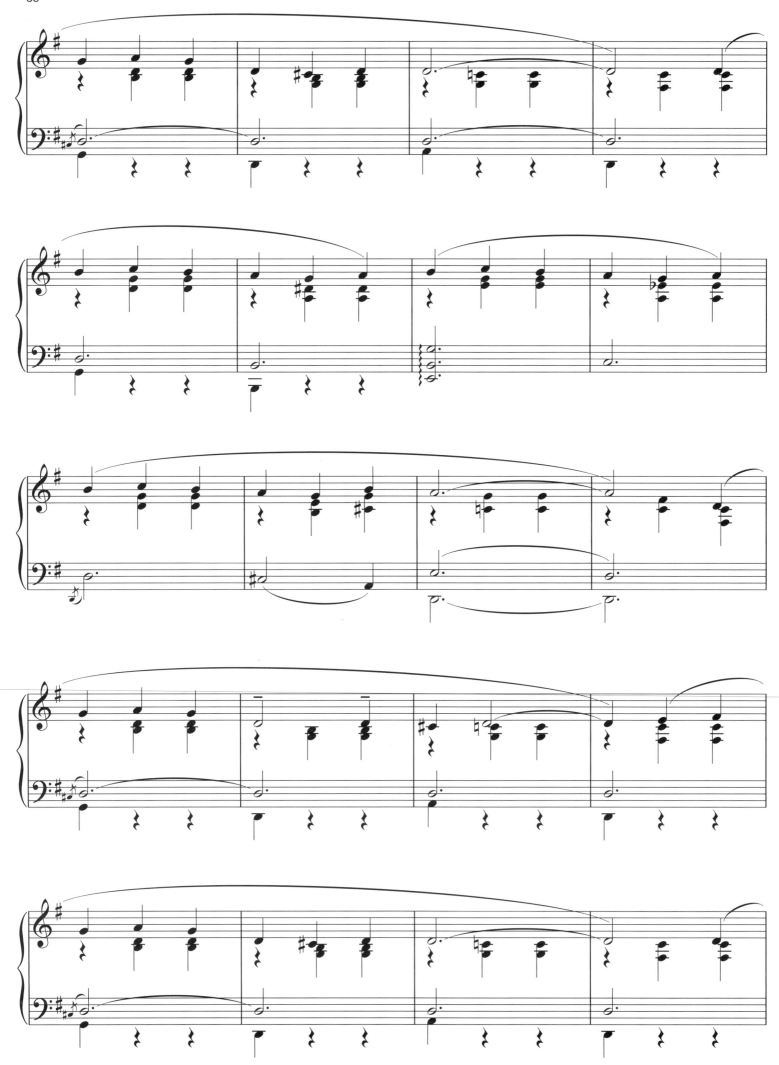

FORREST GUMP – MAIN TITLE
(Feather Theme)
from the Paramount Motion Picture FORREST GUMP

Music by ALAN SILVESTRI

8va--------

f

(lightly)

GABRIEL'S OBOE
from the Motion Picture THE MISSION

Music by ENNIO MORRICONE

Slowly, expressively

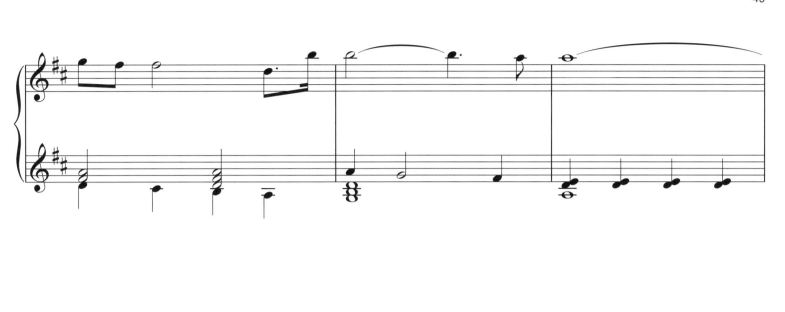

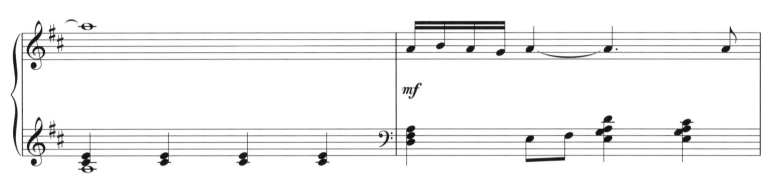

GOLDEN SLUMBERS

Words and Music by JOHN LENNON
and PAUL McCARTNEY

Moderately

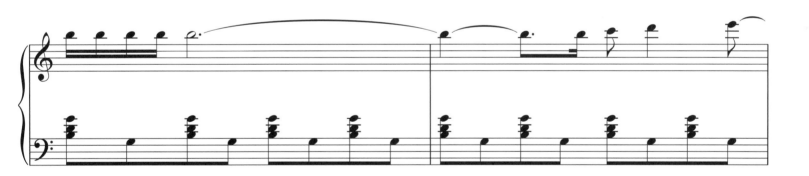

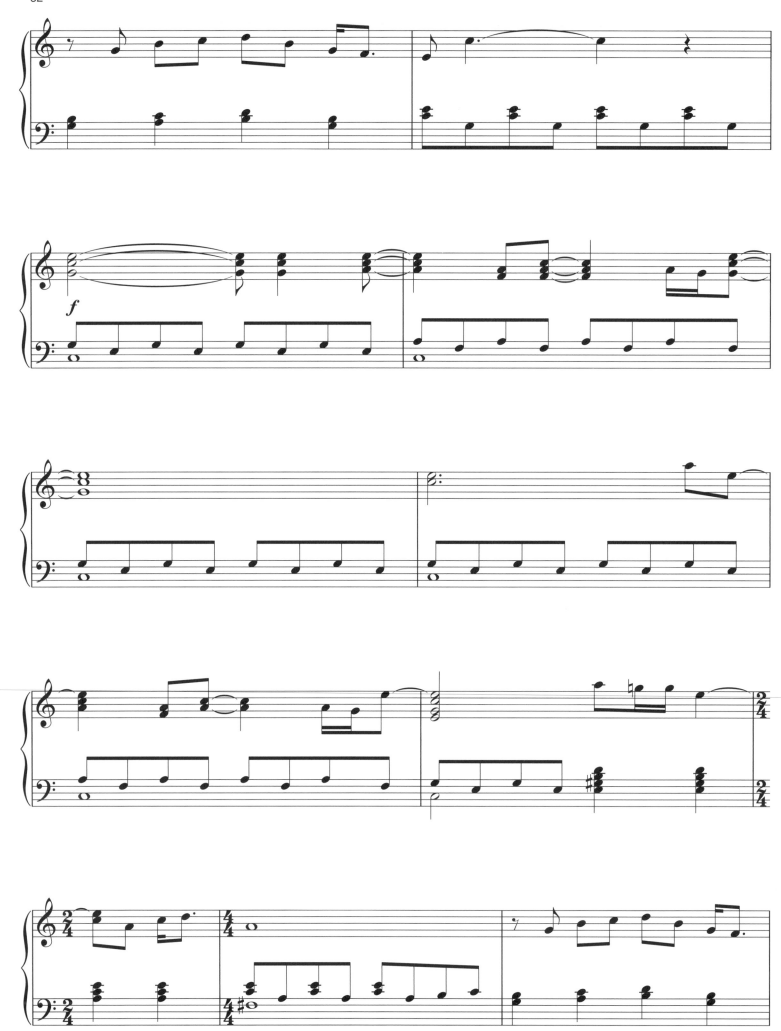

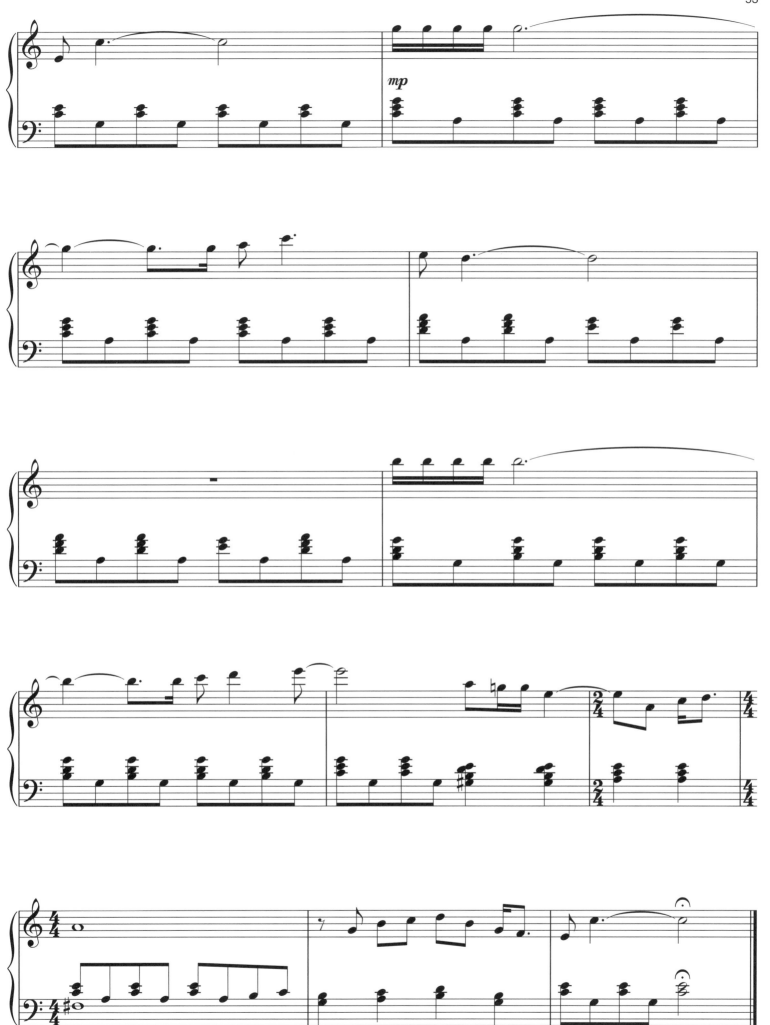

GONNA FLY NOW
Theme from ROCKY

By BILL CONTI, AYN ROBBINS
and CAROL CONNORS

Moderately, not too fast

HALLELUJAH

Words and Music by
LEONARD COHEN

Moderately slow, in 2

THE GOOD, THE BAD AND THE UGLY

(Main Title)

from THE GOOD, THE BAD AND THE UGLY

By ENNIO MORRICONE

Brightly, but not too fast

To Coda ⊕

D.S. al Coda

CODA

HABANERA
from CARMEN

By GEORGES BIZET

Allegretto quasi Andantino

I'M ALWAYS CHASING RAINBOWS

Words by JOSEPH McCARTHY
Music by HARRY CARROLL

Moderately flowing

HIGHLAND CATHEDRAL

By MICHAEL KORB
and ULRICH ROEVER

Stately March, in 2

With pedal

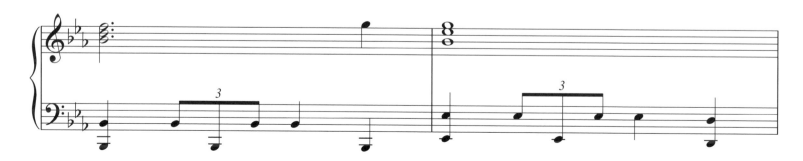

To Coda

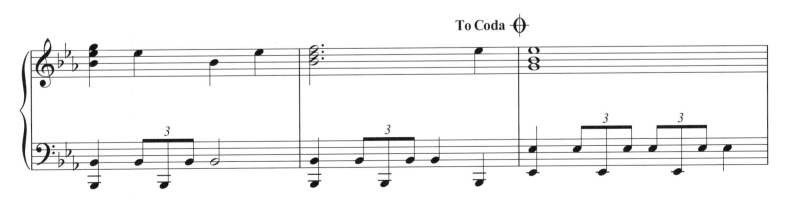

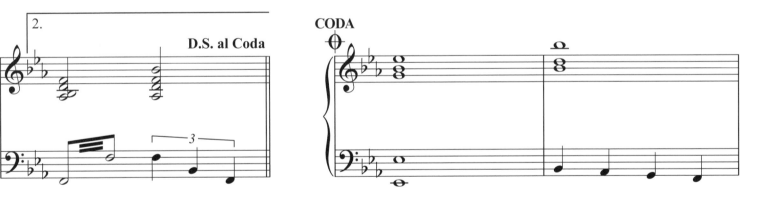

I HAVE A DREAM
from MAMMA MIA!

Words and Music by BENNY ANDERSSON
and BJÖRN ULVAEUS

Moderate Ballad

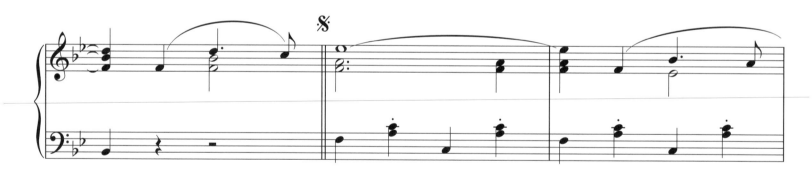

To Coda ⊕

IN MY LIFE

Words and Music by JOHN LENNON
and PAUL McCARTNEY

Moderately

With pedal

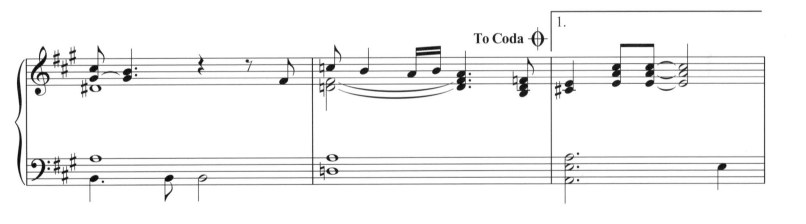

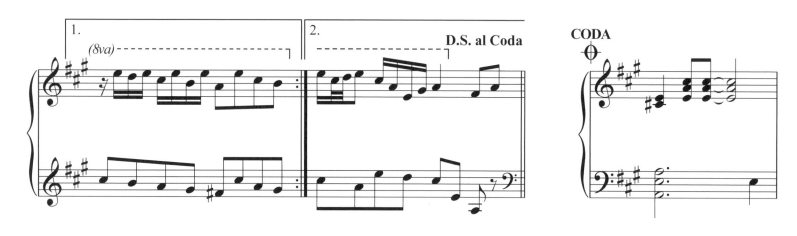

LOVE IS BLUE
(L'amour est bleu)

English Lyric by BRYAN BLACKBURN
Original French Lyric by PIERRE COUR
Music by ANDRE POPP

LA CALIFFA

Music by ENNIO MORRICONE

THE LAST FAREWELL

Words and Music by RONALD WEBSTER
and ROGER WHITTAKER

MORNING HAS BROKEN

Words by ELEANOR FARJEON
Music by CAT STEVENS

94

LULLABYE
(Goodnight, My Angel)

Words and Music by
BILLY JOEL

Rubato, gently

OLYMPIC FANFARE AND THEME

Commissioned by the 1984 Los Angeles Olympic Organizing Committee

Music by JOHN WILLIAMS

Maestoso

MEMORY
from CATS

Music by ANDREW LLOYD WEBBER
Text by TREVOR NUNN after T.S. ELIOT

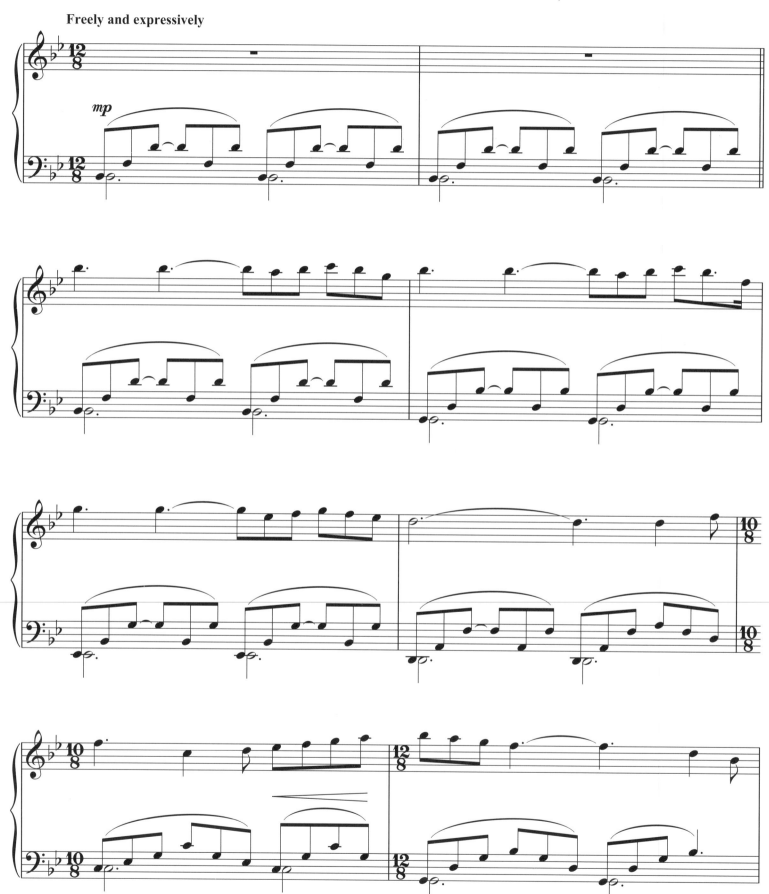

THE MISSION
from the Motion Picture THE MISSION

Music by ENNIO MORRICONE

Moderately slow, with expression

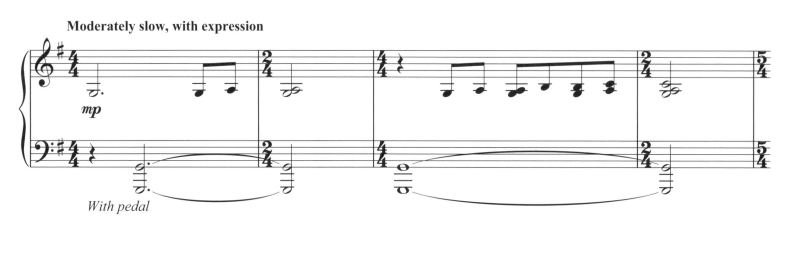

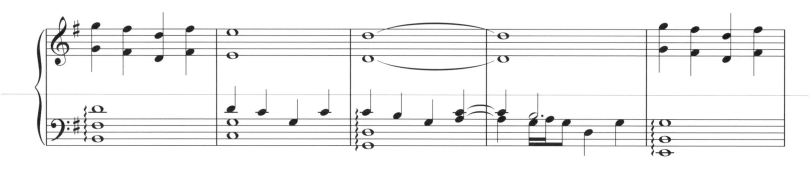

NOT ABOUT ANGELS
from the Motion Picture Soundtrack THE FAULT IN OUR STARS

Words and Music by
JASMINE VAN DEN BOGAERDE

OBLIVION

By ASTOR PIAZZOLLA

Moderately slow

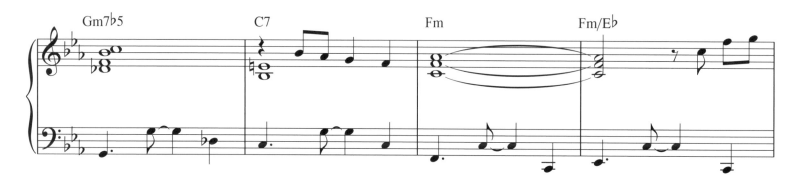

ORINOCO FLOW

Music by ENYA
Words by ROMA RYAN

PETER AND THE WOLF MARCH

By SERGEI PROKOFIEV

Brightly, in 2

RAIDERS MARCH

from the Paramount Motion Picture RAIDERS OF THE LOST ARK

Music by JOHN WILLIAMS

SHENANDOAH

American Folksong

OVER THE RAINBOW
from THE WIZARD OF OZ

Music by HAROLD ARLEN
Lyric by E.Y. "YIP" HARBURG

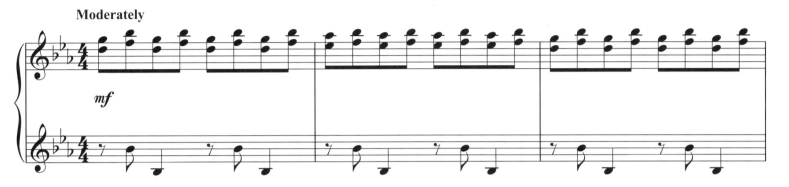

(Theme from)
A SUMMER PLACE
from A SUMMER PLACE

Words by MACK DISCANT
Music by MAX STEINER

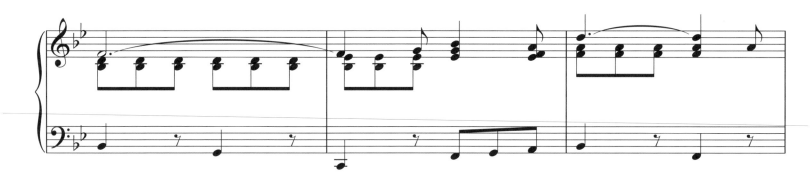

STRANGER ON THE SHORE

from FLAMINGO KID

Words by ROBERT MELLIN
Music by ACKER BILK

Moderate, relaxed feel

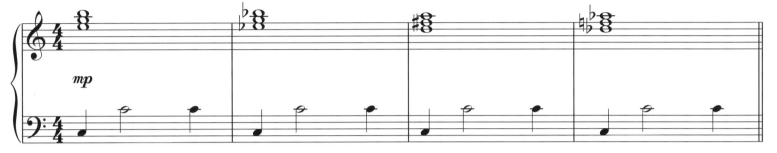

With pedal

A WALK IN THE BLACK FOREST
(I Walk with You)

Words by KAL MANN
Music by HORST JANKOWSKI

Lightly, in 2

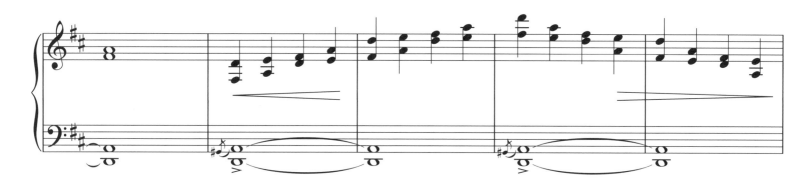

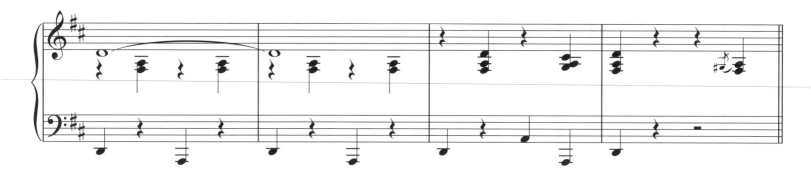

150

THE TOY TRUMPET

By RAYMOND SCOTT

cresc. poco a poco

WALTZ IN D-FLAT MAJOR
("Minute Waltz")

By FRYDERYK CHOPIN
Op. 64, No. 1

WALTZ OF THE FLOWERS
from THE NUTCRACKER

By PYOTR IL'YICH TCHAIKOVSKY

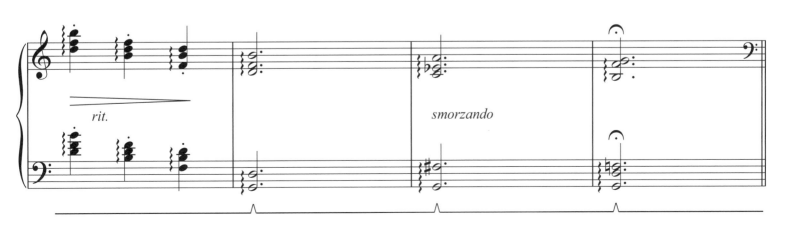

WONDERLAND BY NIGHT

Words by LINCOLN CHASE
Music by KLAUSS GUNTER-NEUMAN